The State
Of
CONFUSION
2024

The State of Confusion 2024

Thomas Paine Jr.

ISBN: 9781088131558

Proudly Printed In The USA

The Ten Commandments
The Ten Commandments
My fellow Americans
I can't lead America with
ancient Ideas.

I have disregarded my oath of office to defend you against all threats both foreign and domestic.

I have opened up our southern border. I let everybody in. The good, the bad, the drug dealers, the terrorists; They are all welcome!

If and only if they vote for me!

I came to this office to get you
through one of the toughest periods
in history.
I printed and gave away millions of
dollars. Remember... That's the only
reason you would actually vote for me
in the first place.

By doing this, I caused a bigger problem than a pandemic. I caused inflation.
I am the reason that you can no longer afford groceries!

I caused the over inflated prices on your house note, your car note, and your credit cards.
That is, if you still have them.
BANK
OWNED

I even caused the price you pay at the pump to rise.

Thanks to me...

Your energy bill is higher
than it has ever been!

But, I didn't stop there.
My administration have been replacing the family farms. The fields that were once filled with cattle, sheep, and grain have all been replaced.

Those fields, you know the ones that you played in as children, now are home to the most beautiful solar farms that the world has ever seen.
Who needs to eat anyway!

Thanks to me... unemployment is at a 50-year low.

Don't tell anyone, but it is only because their benefits ran out.

For years, all that I've heard from my Republican friends is that China's on the rise and America is falling behind. They've got it backwards!

Or, do they?

MADE IN CHINA

Buy American!

That's my motto!

That's why everything from toilet paper to the cars we drive are stamped "made in China".

My predecessor failed to buy American. He only added tariffs on imports from China. What good would that do?

I am also expanding the grip of Obama-Care. The cost of your perscriptions will be lowered.
Instead of a higher price for the life saving drugs that you need, your insurance company can now deny your claim all together. R.I.P.

The Biden
Guide To Screw
America
We need to stop denying Americas
core values. Banning Books! It's
Wrong! Fill the school libraries with
garbage! Let's make history!

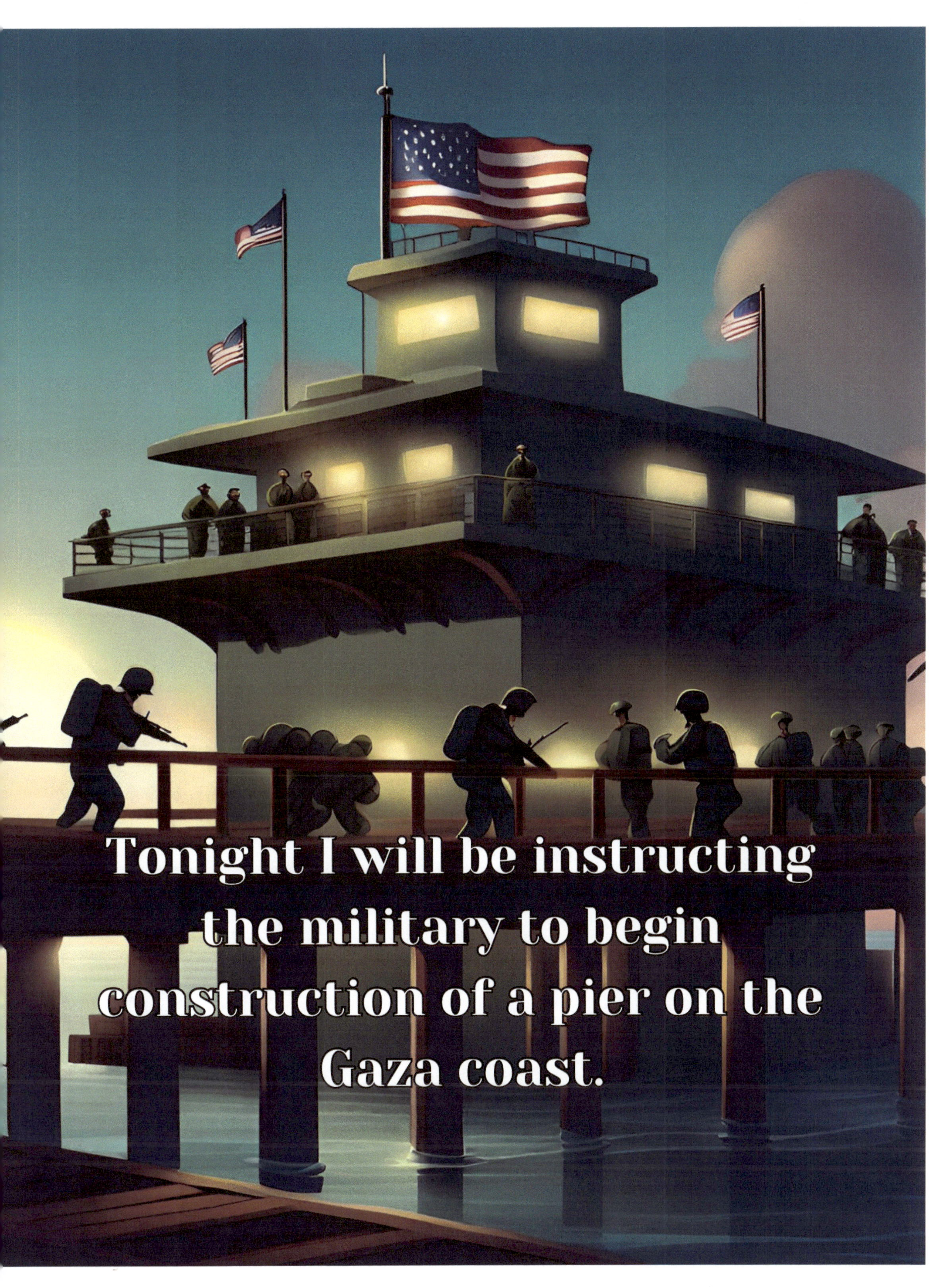
Tonight I will be instructing the military to begin construction of a pier on the Gaza coast.

This temporary pier would enable a massive increase of humanitarian aid to be brought in to Gaza.

Protecting and saving innocent
lives has to be a priority.
At least it has to be overseas.

I say to you!
The innocent lives of un-
born American babies have
no place! Roe vs Wade must
not be overturned!

Furthermore,

It is because of you America is coming back!

It is because of you the
future of America is
brighter!

And it's because of me that
the state of our union is
confusion.

This is why...
On election Day...
Our only hope...

Vote
Donald J. Trump
for President!

God Bless
America!

www.ingramcontent.com/pod-product-compliance
Lightning Source LLC
Chambersburg PA
CBHW042131030726
47599CB00002B/429

* 9 7 8 1 0 8 8 1 3 1 5 5 8 *